W9-BIM-354

STEM *trailblazer* BIOS

MARS SCIENCE LAB ENGINEER

DIANA TRUJILLO

KARI CORNELL

Lerner Publications
Minneapolis

For Will and Theo, the sky's the limit

Copyright © 2016 by Lerner Publishing Group, Inc.

Note to readers: This biography is not authorized or licensed but has been carefully researched and fact-checked against a combination of primary and secondary sources. In addition, all scientific information in the book has been vetted by a subject-area expert.

All rights reserved. International copyright secured. No part of this book may be reproduced, stored in a retrieval system, or transmitted in any form or by any means—electronic, mechanical, photocopying, recording, or otherwise—without the prior written permission of Lerner Publishing Group, Inc., except for the inclusion of brief quotations in an acknowledged review.

Lerner Publications Company
A division of Lerner Publishing Group, Inc.
241 First Avenue North
Minneapolis, MN 55401 USA

For reading levels and more information, look up this title at www.lernerbooks.com.

Content Consultant: James Flaten, Ph.D., U of MN Aerospace Engineering and Mechanics Department, Associate Director of NASA's Minnesota Space Grant Consortium

Library of Congress Cataloging-in-Publication Data

Cornell, Kari, author.
Mars science lab engineer Diana Trujillo / Kari Cornell.
     pages cm. — (STEM trailblazer bios)
     Audience: Ages 7–11.
     Audience: Grades 4 to 6.
     ISBN 978-1-4677-9530-2 (lb : alk. paper) — ISBN 978-1-4677-9721-4 (pb : alk. paper)
     ISBN 978-1-4677-9722-1 (eb pdf)
     1. Trujillo, Diana—Juvenile literature. 2. Women engineers—United States—Biography—Juvenile literature. 3. Engineers—United States—Biography—Juvenile literature. 4. Hispanic American women—Biography—Juvenile literature. 5. Curiosity (Spacecraft)—Juvenile literature. 6. Mars (Planet)—Exploration—Juvenile literature. I. Title. II. Series: STEM trailblazer bios.
     TA157.5.C67 2016
     629.43092—dc23   2015013835

Manufactured in the United States of America
1 – BP – 12/31/15

The images in this book are used with the permission of: Courtesy Diana Trujillo, p. 4; NASA, pp. 5, 17; © David Alejandro Rendón/Wikimedia Commons (CC BY-SA 3.0), p. 6; © EFE/Iván Mejía, p. 9; © iStockphoto.com/Denis Tangney Jr., pp. 10, 12; © RosaBetancourt 0 people images/Alamy, p. 11; © CNET, pp. 14, 22; NASA/Desiree Stover, p. 15; NASA/JPL-Caltech/Cornell Univ./Arizona State Univ., p. 19; NASA/JPL-Caltech/MSSS, p. 20; NASA/JPL-Caltech, pp. 21, 23, 26; NASA/Bill Ingalls, p. 25; © Vincent Sandoval/Getty Images, p. 27.

Front cover: Courtesy Diana Trujillo; NASA/JPL-Caltech (background).

Main body text set in Adrianna Regular 13/22. Typeface provided by Chank.

CONTENTS

CHAPTER 1
Touch the Stars   4

CHAPTER 2
A Whole New World   10

CHAPTER 3
Working for NASA   14

CHAPTER 4
Leading a Team   22

Timeline   29
Source Notes   30
Glossary   30
Further Information   31
Index   32

Diana Trujillo decided at the age of eleven that one day she would work for NASA.

TOUCH THE STARS

As a child, Diana Trujillo gazed at the stars and the sky. More than anything, she wished she could reach out and touch them. She wanted to know more about what was in outer space.

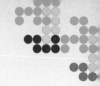

When Diana was eleven, she learned about the National Aeronautics and Space Administration (NASA) at school. She learned that NASA built rockets and sent astronauts into space. Her school gave her a NASA sticker. Diana loved the sticker's design. And she knew that one day she wanted to wear the logo that appeared on the sticker. She wanted to work at NASA.

When Diana was a girl, the Mir Space Station (below) was the shining star of space exploration. Its name can be read in English as "world," "peace," or "village."

THE EARLY YEARS

Diana grew up in Cali, Colombia, in the 1980s and 1990s. As a young girl, Diana liked figuring out how things worked. She spent hours at the library reading books. She also played outside and explored nature. She learned to swim, dance, and roller-skate. When she swam and danced, Diana paid attention to how her body moved through water and air. When she roller-skated, she wondered what made the wheels of her skates roll along the sidewalk.

Diana's hometown of Cali, Colombia

Diana loved to draw and design too. She loved that even a single line could look different depending on how she drew it. She found art in books and then combined images to make a new design. Diana also spent many hours building things with LEGO bricks alongside her younger brother. They would build their own rocket ships and launching pads, cars, cities, and creatures. Diana thought carefully about how the LEGO bricks could fit together to form different structures.

NASA IN THE 1990s

The 1990s was a very exciting time at NASA. In just ten years, NASA launched more than sixty space shuttle missions—more than twice the number of space shuttles that they had launched in the 1980s. In 1990, the space shuttle *Discovery* carried the Hubble Space Telescope into space. With this telescope, scientists are able to view space in a way they never could from Earth. The next year, NASA began building a space station. In 1997, NASA sent a land explorer called *Sojourner* to Mars. A camera on *Sojourner* took more than 550 photos of the Martian landscape.

MAKING CONNECTIONS

After school, Diana would visit her grandfather, who owned a corner store in a small Colombian village. The store didn't have a cash register, so every time a customer bought something, Diana's grandfather had to do his own math. When Diana visited, her grandfather turned the math into a game. He and Diana raced to see who could add up the prices faster.

Diana's other grandfather owned a company that made parts for cars and machines. When Diana visited, she saw people using math to create new machine parts. But Diana also noticed something else. The **engineers** weren't just using

CHALLENGED BY PHYSICS

In school, Diana's favorite subjects were math, art, and **chemistry**. But she struggled with physics. Physics includes the study of how things move when pushed or pulled in different directions. Diana's mother hired a tutor to help her with physics after school. Though it wasn't easy, Diana worked hard. As an adult, Diana completely overcame her struggles with physics. At NASA, she uses physics every day!

TECH TALK

"I spent so much time as a child trying to connect the dots. My job now allows me to do just that."

—*Diana Trujillo*

math. They were using art too! They used rulers to draw and design parts. Diana realized she could use her love of math and her love of drawing at the same time.

Diana's hard work in math and science would pay off later when she worked on the design of the Mars *Curiosity* rover.

Chapter 2

Trujillo believed in herself enough to move to Miami, Florida, although she didn't speak English.

A WHOLE NEW WORLD

In 2000, Diana graduated from high school. That same year, she packed her bags and moved to Miami, Florida, all by herself. She wanted to follow her dream of someday working at NASA. Moving to a new country was exciting, but it was scary too. Diana didn't speak any English. And she didn't have any family members nearby to help her.

Diana enrolled at Miami Dade College. Before she could take math or science classes, she had to learn English. For two years, she took only English classes. She worked hard, stayed focused, and learned quickly. But learning a new language was not easy. When Diana needed a break, she stopped by the math department. She really missed doing math, so she asked if she could borrow a textbook. Thinking through math problems helped Diana relax.

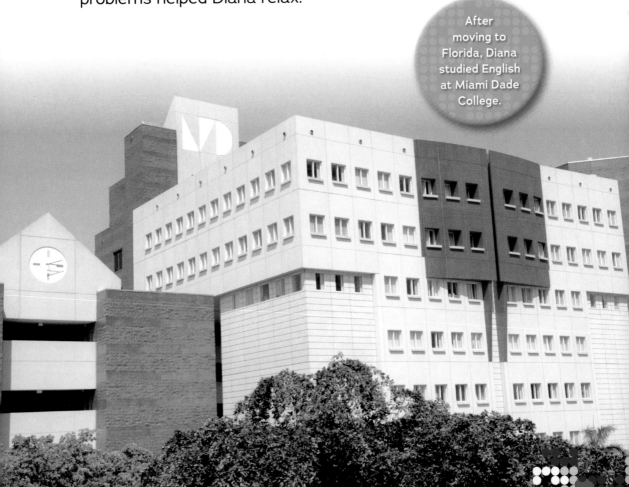

After moving to Florida, Diana studied English at Miami Dade College.

As the year went on, Trujillo started spending more and more time in the math department. The college's math teachers noticed. They thought Trujillo could help other students. Soon the department hired Trujillo to work as a math tutor. She was able to improve her English and keep her math skills sharp at the same time.

Trujillo studied aerospace and mechanical engineering at the University of Florida.

STEPPING INTO SCIENCE

Once Trujillo could speak English fluently, she began to take other classes. She loaded her schedule with math classes and took some space science classes as well. Trujillo enjoyed Miami Dade, but she knew she would need a four-year degree if she wanted to work at NASA. In 2002, Trujillo enrolled at the University of Florida, a four-year college several hours away. She decided to study **aerospace** and **mechanical engineering**. This meant she would learn about designing and building airplanes and rockets. Trujillo was one step closer to her dream!

At the university, Trujillo began to see how she could use science to solve everyday problems. In one of her classes, Trujillo worked with a professor to help solve knee pain in people with **arthritis**. Trujillo and her professor studied the way the leg and knee move when people walk. They learned that by slightly changing the way a person walks, the knee stopped hurting. Trujillo loved coming up with solutions that helped people.

Chapter 3

Trujillo's talent and hard work meant early success at NASA.

WORKING FOR NASA

In 2006, Trujillo applied to and was accepted into a NASA Academy, a ten-week program that would allow her to learn about NASA and visit NASA laboratories. She would also get to do research with NASA scientists.

That summer, she traveled to Goddard Space Flight Center in Maryland to attend the academy. As a group, the students attending the academy flew all around the country visiting many of NASA's research centers. The students met many people who worked for NASA. Trujillo was excited to find out that there were many jobs at NASA, but she was also disappointed. Few of the scientists were women, and even fewer were Latino. But this didn't crush her dream.

Scientists work on a telescope at NASA's Goddard Space Flight Center.

TECH TALK

"[Success] is not about whether you are male or female. It's about what you have in your head and in your heart that makes it happen."

—*Diana Trujillo*

Instead, she decided she wanted to work for NASA so that she could be a role model for other women and immigrants.

During her time at the academy, Trujillo helped Brian Roberts, a professor at the University of Maryland, research space and gravity. Using a space center that Roberts had set up underwater, the pair explored how robots operated while floating as they would in space. The research would help NASA build robots for the shuttles they sent to space.

At the end of the academy, Roberts asked Trujillo if she would continue doing research with him. She agreed. That fall, Trujillo transferred to the University of Maryland. Just a few months later, she graduated from the university with a degree in aerospace engineering.

After graduating, Trujillo began working at NASA. She was finally living her childhood dream. With a team of scientists, Trujillo started working on the Constellation Program, which focused on sending astronauts to the moon.

Trujillo's first job at NASA was with a program that sent astronauts to the moon.

But Trujillo didn't work on the Constellation Program for long. In 2008, Trujillo joined the Mars *Curiosity* rover project at NASA's Jet Propulsion Lab (JPL). A rover is a vehicle that scientists use to explore the surface of planets. *Curiosity* would explore the surface of the planet Mars. It would take photos and collect rock samples for research. Back on Earth, scientists and engineers would use computers to watch and control the rover.

LIFE ON MARS

Why does NASA spend time on Mars? One reason is to see if humans could ever live there. Another is to see if there ever was life on Mars. To find out, scientists study the rocks and soil of the planet. Think about life on Earth. Earth's rocks and soil hold fossils and other clues to the history of life on this planet. Scientists believe that the same kind of evidence may exist in the rocks on Mars. To find out, *Curiosity* collects samples of rocks so scientists can study them.

At JPL, Trujillo worked with a team of engineers who were trying to figure out a way to collect samples of rocks from the surface of Mars. The team faced a challenge, though. A fine, red dust covers nearly everything on Mars. This made it hard to get clean samples of rocks.

NASA scientists hoped to learn about Mars by studying the rocks that cover its surface.

Working with other engineers, Trujillo helped design the Dust Removal Tool. The tool, in a circular motion, brushes away the red dust that covers the surface of Mars. With the dust removed, scientists can see the rock underneath and decide whether to drill into it.

A patch of rock cleaned by the first use of the rover's Dust Removal Tool

Trujillo sits in front of a model of the *Curiosity* rover at NASA.

Chapter 4

Trujillo has become a role model for Latinas interested in science.

LEADING A TEAM

While she was working on the Dust Removal Tool, Trujillo became the team's lead engineer. This meant that she wasn't just helping to design the tool—she was leading the whole team of engineers! Though the tool has a simple job, it wasn't simple to design. The team needed to build a mechanical arm that would hold a stainless steel wire-bristled brush. The team had to put together just the right parts to move the arm and allow the brush to swing in the correct direction. NASA also needed to use radios to send instructions to the tool through outer space. After forty-three tests, the team finally found the right combination. The design of the Dust Removal Tool was complete.

Scientists test *Curiosity*, the rover that used the Dust Removal Tool developed by Trujillo and her team.

CURIOSITY

Curiosity was built by Honeybee Robotics of New York and cost $2.5 billion. The rover can take samples of the soil. Scientists test soil to see if small life-forms, called **microbes**, ever existed on Mars. *Curiosity* also takes pictures using a camera called a Mars Hand Lens Imager (MAHLI). Like the Dust Removal Tool, this camera is mounted on *Curiosity*'s robotic arm.

THE LANDING

Curiosity was launched from Cape Canaveral in Florida on November 26, 2011. After traveling for eight and a half months and 352 million miles (566 million kilometers), the craft landed on Mars on August 5, 2012. That day, Trujillo and her team at NASA took a break from the long hours of testing to celebrate. Everyone at JPL gathered to watch the landing on big movie screens. Many held their breath until *Curiosity* was safely on the surface of Mars. When *Curiosity* finally landed, the room filled with the sound of applause and cheers. *Curiosity* had made it to Mars!

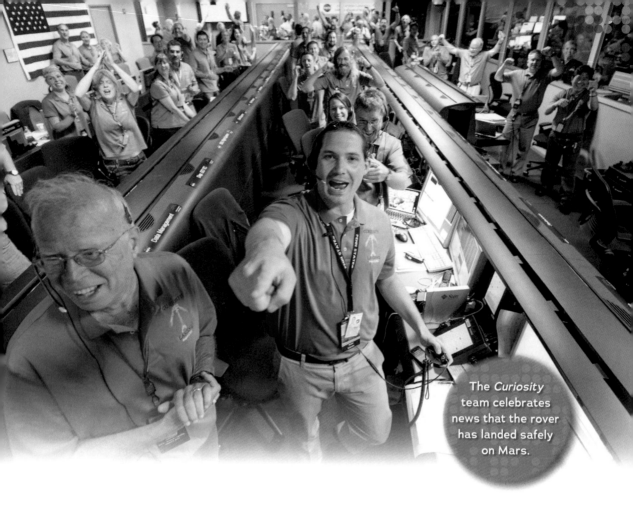

The *Curiosity* team celebrates news that the rover has landed safely on Mars.

For Trujillo, though, more tense moments were still to come. She and her team would keep testing the Dust Removal Tool until everything worked perfectly. Months later, on January 6, 2013, the Dust Removal Tool was used for the first time on Mars. The brush cleared the red dust from the surface of a rock called Ekwir 1. With the dust removed, *Curiosity* could drill for rock samples. Years of testing, fixing, and adjusting had finally paid off!

NASA first tested *Curiosity*'s drill on the surface of Mars on February 2, 2013.

MANAGING *CURIOSITY*

Since the landing, Trujillo has continued to work on the *Curiosity* rover project at JPL. She works as the tactical uplink lead for the rover. This means that she is in charge of making sure all the different parts of the rover are working together. If two different teams send instructions to *Curiosity* at the same time, Trujillo makes sure they don't interfere with each other. She makes sure the rover and mission are safe.

Trujillo with her husband, who is also a graduate of the NASA academy.

Trujillo also mentors new scientists at NASA. She talks to students in schools too. Trujillo believes that just as she found a connection between art and math, everyone can find a connection between their passions and a career in science or math.

TECH TALK

"My advice for students is to pick a topic you like, study a topic you like, and then you will see a connection. Because everything uses math!"

—*Diana Trujillo*

TIMELINE

1983

Diana Trujillo is born in Cali, Colombia.

2000

At the age of seventeen, Trujillo graduates from high school and moves to the United States to attend Miami Dade College. She studies English there for two years.

2002

Trujillo enrolls at the University of Florida, where she studies aerospace and mechanical engineering.

2006

Trujillo attends the NASA Academy at Goddard Space Flight Center in Maryland. She transfers to the University of Maryland to do research with Brian Roberts.

2008

Trujillo is hired to work on NASA's Constellation Program.

2009

Trujillo begins working on the *Curiosity* rover project at NASA's Jet Propulsion Lab in Pasadena, California.

2012

On August 5, the *Curiosity* rover safely lands on Mars.

2013

On January 6, the *Curiosity* rover uses the Dust Removal Tool for the first time on a Martian rock called Ekwir 1.

SOURCE NOTES

9 Diana Trujillo, interview with the author, March 12, 2015.

16 Ibid.

28 Ibid.

GLOSSARY

aerospace
the design or operation of aircraft or spacecraft

arthritis
a disease that causes pain in joints such as the elbows and knees

chemistry
the study of the chemical makeup of living things

engineers
people who use science to design, build, and improve things

mechanical engineering
using physics and materials to create machines

microbes
living things that are too small to be seen without a microscope

FURTHER INFORMATION

BOOKS

O'Brien, Patrick. *You Are the First Kid on Mars.* New York: G. P. Putnam, 2009. Read about what it might be like to be an astronaut on Mars.

Rusch, Elizabeth. *The Mighty Mars Rovers: The Incredible Adventures of Spirit and Opportunity.* New York: Houghton Mifflin Books for Children, 2012. Find out more about the Mars rovers that came before *Curiosity*.

Storad, Conrad J. *Mars.* Minneapolis: Lerner Publications, 2010. Explore the characteristics of Mars and its place in the solar system.

WEBSITES

NASA: I Am Diana Trujillo
http://mars.nasa.gov/people/info.cfm?id=22822
Find out more about Diana Trujillo and her work at NASA.

NASA: Mars Exploration
http://mars.nasa.gov
Keep up with the latest news of *Curiosity*'s findings on Mars.

Smithsonian Latino Virtual Museum: Diana Trujillo
http://smithsonianlvm.tumblr.com/post/112707531602 /celebrating-latinas-in-stem-diana-trujillo-nasa
Read about Diana Trujillo's accomplishments at the Jet Propulsion Laboratory.

LERNER
SOURCE

Expand learning beyond the printed book. Download free, complementary educational resources for this book from our website, www.lerneresource.com.

INDEX

aerospace engineering, 13, 16, 29

astronaut, 5, 17

Cali, Colombia, 6, 29

Constellation Program, 17–18, 29

Curiosity, 18, 24–25, 26, 29

Discovery, 7

Dust Removal Tool, 20, 22–23, 24, 25, 29

Ekwir 1, 25, 29

English, 11–12, 13, 29

Goddard Space Flight Center, 15, 29

Honeybee Robotics, 24

Hubble Space Telescope, 7

Jet Propulsion Lab (JPL), 18–19, 24, 26, 29

Mars Hand Lens Imager (MAHLI), 24

mechanical engineering, 13, 29

Miami Dade College, 11–12, 29

NASA Academy, 14–15, 16, 29

physics, 8

research, 14–15, 16, 18, 29

Roberts, Brian, 16, 29

Sojourner, 7

University of Florida, 13, 29

University of Maryland, 16, 29

ABOUT THE AUTHOR

Kari Cornell is a freelance writer and editor who lives with her husband, two sons, and dog in Minneapolis, Minnesota. One of her favorite things to do is to write about people who've found a way to do what they love. When she's not writing, she likes tinkering in the garden, cooking, and making something clever out of nothing. Find out more about her work at karicornell.wordpress.com.